Chicken Enchiladas Recipes

A Flavorful Collection of Delicious Chicken Enchiladas for Every Occasion

While every precaution has been taken in the preparation of this book, the publisher assumes no responsibility for errors or omissions, or for damages resulting from the use of the information contained herein.

CHICKEN ENCHILADAS RECIPES

First edition. December 8, 2023.

ISBN: 979-8223869825

Written by john ahmad.

Table of Contents

John Ahmad

Chapter 1: Introduction to Chicken Enchiladas

The History and Origin of Enchiladas

Enchiladas, a beloved Mexican dish, have a rich history that dates back to ancient Mesoamerican civilizations. The concept of wrapping fillings in tortillas can be traced to the Aztecs and Mayans, who used corn tortillas to create portable meals. These early versions of enchiladas were filled with a variety of ingredients, including fish, beans, and meat.

As Spanish colonialists arrived in the Americas, they introduced new ingredients such as dairy products and various meats. This led to the fusion of indigenous and European culinary traditions, giving rise to the enchiladas we know today. The word "enchilada" itself comes from the Spanish word "enchilar," meaning "to season with chili."

Over time, enchiladas became an integral part of Mexican cuisine, with each region putting its own spin on the dish. In central Mexico, traditional red enchilada sauce, made from dried chili peppers, became a staple. In coastal regions, seafood-filled enchiladas became popular. The dish continued to evolve, adapting to local ingredients and preferences.

The Versatility of Chicken Enchiladas

Chicken enchiladas offer a canvas of flavors and textures that can be customized to suit a wide range of tastes. From classic to creative, the possibilities are nearly endless. Here's a glimpse into the versatility that chicken enchiladas bring to the table:

Flavor Profiles: Whether you prefer smoky, spicy, or tangy flavors, chicken enchiladas can be tailored to satisfy your palate. The combination of spices, herbs, and seasonings allows for a multitude of taste experiences.

Sauce Variations: The sauce is the heart of any enchilada dish. Traditional red and vibrant green sauces offer distinct tastes, while creamy sauces add richness. Experiment with sauces inspired by different cuisines to create unique and memorable flavors.

Chicken Choices: The choice of chicken preparation greatly influences the overall character of your enchiladas. Opt for tender shredded chicken, succulent grilled chicken, or even marinated chicken for an extra burst of flavor.

Tortilla Options: The type of tortilla you choose can impact the texture and taste of your enchiladas. Corn tortillas bring a traditional touch, while flour tortillas lend a softer bite. Explore various tortilla sizes and thicknesses to find your ideal match.

Throughout this cookbook, we'll explore a diverse array of chicken enchilada recipes, each highlighting a distinct combination of ingredients and techniques. From cherished classics to innovative fusions, get ready to embark on a flavorful journey that celebrates the heritage and adaptability of chicken enchiladas.

Chapter 2: Kitchen Essentials for Enchilada Making

Must-Have Ingredients

Creating delicious chicken enchiladas requires a well-stocked kitchen with essential ingredients that form the foundation of flavor. From vibrant sauces to succulent fillings, here's a breakdown of the must-have ingredients for crafting perfect enchiladas:

1. Tortillas: Choose between corn or flour tortillas, based on your preference. Corn tortillas offer a traditional flavor, while flour tortillas provide a softer texture.

2. Chicken: opt for boneless, skinless chicken breasts or thighs. They serve as the protein-rich centerpiece of your enchiladas.

3. Cheese: Shredded cheese, such as cheddar, Monterey Jack, or queso fresco, adds a delightful creaminess and depth of flavor.

4. Enchilada Sauce: Stock up on store-bought red and green enchilada sauces, or experiment with making your own from dried or fresh chili peppers.

5. Aromatics: Onions, garlic, and various spices like cumin, paprika, and chili powder enhance the overall taste of your enchiladas.

6. Fresh Herbs: Cilantro and fresh oregano provide a burst of freshness and herbal notes to balance the richness.

7. Cooking Oil: Use a neutral oil like vegetable or canola oil for sautéing and frying tortillas.

8. Seasonings: Salt and pepper are essential for seasoning chicken and adjusting flavors.

9. Toppings: Gather toppings such as sour cream, diced tomatoes, sliced jalapeños, and sliced avocado to customize your enchiladas.

Essential Cooking Utensils

Equipping your kitchen with the right tools simplifies the enchilada-making process and ensures a seamless cooking experience. Here are the essential cooking utensils you'll need:

1. Skillet or Saucepan: A skillet or saucepan is essential for sautéing chicken and simmering sauces.

2. Baking Dish: Choose an appropriately sized baking dish to assemble and bake your enchiladas.

3. Mixing Bowls: Have various sizes of mixing bowls on hand for combining ingredients and tossing fillings.

4. Tongs: Tongs are handy for flipping tortillas and transferring chicken without damaging its texture.

5. Wooden Spoon or Spatula: Use a wooden spoon or spatula for stirring sauces and mixing fillings.

6. Grater: A cheese grater is useful for shredding cheese and vegetables.

7. Cutting Board and Knife: A sturdy cutting board and sharp knife are essential for chopping and preparing ingredients.

8. Basting Brush: Use a basting brush to coat tortillas with sauce before rolling them.

9. Aluminum Foil: Aluminum foil helps cover and protect enchiladas while baking.

10. Serving Utensils: Ensure you have serving utensils like spatulas, ladles, and forks for dishing out enchiladas.

11. Blender or Food Processor: If making homemade sauces, a blender or food processor is useful for achieving a smooth consistency.

With these essential ingredients and cooking utensils at your disposal, you're well-equipped to dive into the world of chicken enchiladas. In the upcoming chapters, we'll explore a variety of mouthwatering recipes that showcase the beauty of combining these elements to create unforgettable dishes.

Chapter 3: Classic Chicken Enchiladas

Traditional Red Enchilada Sauce

A cornerstone of classic chicken enchiladas is the rich and flavorful red enchilada sauce. This traditional sauce is made from a blend of dried chili peppers, creating a balance of smoky, sweet, and spicy notes. Let's dive into crafting this timeless sauce:

Ingredients:

- 3 dried ancho chili peppers
- 2 dried guajillo chili peppers
- 2 cups hot water
- 1 small onion, roughly chopped
- 3 cloves garlic
- 1 teaspoon ground cumin
- 1 teaspoon dried oregano
- 1/2 teaspoon ground coriander
- 1/2 teaspoon cocoa powder (optional)
- 1 tablespoon vegetable oil
- Salt and pepper to taste

Instructions:

1. Remove the stems and seeds from the dried chili peppers. Tear them into smaller pieces.
2. In a dry skillet over medium heat, lightly toast the chili pepper pieces for about 1-2 minutes until fragrant. Be cautious not to burn them.

3. Transfer the toasted chili peppers to a bowl and cover them with hot water. Let them soak for about 15-20 minutes until softened.
4. In a blender or food processor, combine the soaked chili peppers, chopped onion, garlic, ground cumin, dried oregano, ground coriander, cocoa powder (if using), and a pinch of salt and pepper.
5. Blend the mixture until smooth, gradually adding some of the soaking liquid to achieve the desired consistency.
6. In a saucepan, heat the vegetable oil over medium heat. Pour the blended sauce into the pan and simmer for about 10-15 minutes, stirring occasionally, to develop the flavors.
7. Adjust the seasoning with more salt and pepper if needed. Strain the sauce through a fine mesh sieve for a smoother texture, if desired.
8. Your classic red enchilada sauce is now ready to be used in your enchilada recipes. Set aside until assembly.

Shredded Chicken Filling

The tender and succulent shredded chicken filling is a key component of classic chicken enchiladas. Prepare this versatile filling to create a satisfying and flavorful center for your enchiladas:

Ingredients:

- 2 boneless, skinless chicken breasts
- 1 teaspoon cumin
- 1 teaspoon paprika
- 1/2 teaspoon garlic powder
- Salt and pepper to taste
- 1 tablespoon vegetable oil

Instructions:

1. Preheat your oven to 375°F (190°C).
2. Rub the chicken breasts with cumin, paprika, garlic powder, salt, and pepper.
3. In an oven-safe skillet, heat the vegetable oil over medium-high heat. Add the seasoned chicken breasts and sear them for about 2-3 minutes on each side until lightly browned.
4. Transfer the skillet to the preheated oven and bake the chicken for 20-25 minutes or until fully cooked and no longer pink in the center.
5. Once cooked, remove the chicken from the oven and let it cool slightly. Use two forks to shred the chicken into bite-sized pieces.
6. Your flavorful shredded chicken filling is now ready to be used in your enchiladas.

With your homemade traditional red enchilada sauce and tender shredded chicken filling prepared, you're set to assemble and bake classic chicken enchiladas that pay homage to the time-honored flavors of this beloved dish.

Chapter 4: Green Chile Chicken Enchiladas

Roasted Green Chile Sauce

Green chile chicken enchiladas offer a delightful departure from the classic red sauce, infusing a smoky and tangy flavor into the dish. Crafting a homemade roasted green chile sauce is easier than you might think, and the results are simply sensational:

Ingredients:

- 6-8 medium-sized green chile peppers (such as Anaheim or Hatch)
- 2 cloves garlic, minced
- 1 small onion, chopped
- 2 cups chicken broth
- 1 teaspoon ground cumin
- 1/2 teaspoon dried oregano
- Salt and pepper to taste
- 1 tablespoon vegetable oil

Instructions:

1. Preheat your oven's broiler. Place the green chile peppers on a baking sheet and broil them, turning occasionally, until the skins are charred and blistered. This should take about 10-15 minutes.
2. Transfer the charred chiles to a bowl and cover it with plastic wrap. Allow the chiles to steam for about 10 minutes. This step will help loosen the skins, making them

easier to peel.

3. Once the chiles have steamed, carefully peel off the charred skins and remove the stems and seeds.

4. In a blender or food processor, combine the roasted green chiles, minced garlic, chopped onion, chicken broth, ground cumin, dried oregano, and a pinch of salt and pepper.

5. Blend the mixture until smooth, adding more chicken broth if necessary to achieve your desired consistency.

6. In a saucepan, heat the vegetable oil over medium heat. Pour the blended sauce into the pan and simmer for about 15-20 minutes, stirring occasionally, to meld the flavors.

7. Taste and adjust the seasoning with additional salt and pepper if needed. Your homemade roasted green chile sauce is now ready to be the star of your enchiladas.

Variations of Green Chile Fillings

The filling of your green chile chicken enchiladas is where you can get creative, infusing various ingredients to complement the robust flavors of the green chile sauce. Here are a couple of delicious filling variations to consider:

Option 1: Green Chile Chicken and Cheese Filling

- 2 cups cooked and shredded chicken (rotisserie chicken works well)
- 1 cup shredded Monterey Jack cheese or cheddar cheese
- 1/4 cup chopped fresh cilantro
- Salt and pepper to taste

Option 2: Green Chile and Black Bean Filling

- 1 can (15 ounces) black beans, drained and rinsed
- 1 cup frozen corn, thawed
- 1 cup crumbled queso fresco or feta cheese
- 1/4 cup chopped green onions
- Salt and pepper to taste

Assembly:

1. Preheat your oven to 350°F (175°C).
2. Warm the green chile sauce over low heat while you prepare the tortillas.
3. Soften corn or flour tortillas by wrapping them in a damp paper towel and microwaving for 20-30 seconds.
4. In the center of each tortilla, place a portion of your chosen filling and roll it up tightly. Place the rolled enchiladas seam-side down in a baking dish.
5. Pour the warmed green chile sauce over the enchiladas, ensuring they are evenly coated.
6. Sprinkle additional cheese on top if desired.
7. Bake the enchiladas in the preheated oven for about 20-25 minutes, or until the sauce is bubbly and the cheese is melted and golden.
8. Garnish with fresh cilantro, chopped green onions, and a dollop of sour cream if desired.

With the captivating flavor of roasted green chile sauce and your choice of delightful fillings, these enchiladas are sure to become a new favorite in your culinary repertoire. In the following chapters, we'll continue exploring various enchilada styles that celebrate the vibrant and diverse world of this beloved dish.

Chapter 5: Creamy White Chicken Enchiladas

Rich and Creamy White Sauce

Creamy white chicken enchiladas bring a luxurious twist to the traditional dish, with a velvety sauce that envelops the flavors of the filling. Crafting a rich and luscious white sauce is the key to achieving the signature creaminess that sets these enchiladas apart:

Ingredients:

- 2 tablespoons butter
- 2 tablespoons all-purpose flour
- 2 cups chicken broth
- 1 cup heavy cream
- 1 teaspoon garlic powder
- 1/2 teaspoon onion powder
- 1/2 teaspoon ground cumin
- Salt and white pepper to taste
- 1 cup shredded Monterey Jack cheese or white cheddar cheese

Instructions:

1. In a saucepan, melt the butter over medium heat.
2. Add the flour to the melted butter, stirring constantly to create a smooth roux. Cook the roux for 1-2 minutes, allowing it to slightly deepen in color.
3. Gradually whisk in the chicken broth, ensuring no lumps

form.

4. Reduce the heat to low and add the heavy cream, garlic powder, onion powder, ground cumin, salt, and white pepper. Continue to whisk until the mixture thickens and coats the back of a spoon.

5. Stir in the shredded cheese until it's fully melted and the sauce is smooth and creamy.

6. Taste and adjust the seasoning with additional salt and white pepper if needed. Remove the sauce from heat and set it aside.

Chicken and Cheese Filling

The tender chicken and cheese filling in creamy white chicken enchiladas perfectly complements the richness of the white sauce. Here's how to prepare this delectable filling:

Ingredients:

- 2 cups cooked and shredded chicken (poached or rotisserie)
- 1 cup shredded Monterey Jack cheese or white cheddar cheese
- 1/4 cup chopped fresh cilantro
- Salt and pepper to taste

Assembly:

1. Preheat your oven to 350°F (175°C).
2. Warm the white sauce over low heat while you prepare the tortillas.

3. Soften corn or flour tortillas by wrapping them in a damp paper towel and microwaving for 20-30 seconds.
4. In the center of each tortilla, place a portion of shredded chicken and a sprinkle of shredded cheese and chopped cilantro. Roll up the tortilla tightly around the filling and place it seam-side down in a baking dish.
5. Once all the enchiladas are assembled, pour the warmed white sauce evenly over them.
6. Sprinkle additional cheese on top if desired.
7. Bake the enchiladas in the preheated oven for about 20-25 minutes, or until the sauce is bubbly and the cheese is melted and golden.
8. Garnish with extra chopped cilantro before serving.

Creamy white chicken enchiladas offer a decadent and comforting dining experience, combining the velvety texture of the sauce with the satisfying flavors of the chicken and cheese filling. In the upcoming chapters, we'll explore even more enchanting enchilada variations that cater to diverse tastes and preferences.

Chapter 6: Spicy Chipotle Chicken Enchiladas

Smoky Chipotle Pepper Sauce

Elevate your enchilada game with the bold and fiery flavors of spicy chipotle pepper sauce. This smoky and robust sauce adds a tantalizing kick to your chicken enchiladas, creating a memorable and satisfying dish:

Ingredients:

- 4-6 dried chipotle peppers (adjust to your spice preference)
- 2 cups hot water
- 1 small onion, chopped
- 3 cloves garlic
- 1 cup tomato sauce
- 1 tablespoon adobo sauce (from a can of chipotle peppers in adobo)
- 1 teaspoon ground cumin
- 1/2 teaspoon dried oregano
- Salt and pepper to taste
- 1 tablespoon vegetable oil

Instructions:

1. Remove the stems and seeds from the dried chipotle peppers. Tear them into smaller pieces.
2. In a dry skillet over medium heat, lightly toast the chipotle pepper pieces for about 1-2 minutes until fragrant. Be cautious not to burn them.

3. Transfer the toasted chipotle peppers to a bowl and cover them with hot water. Let them soak for about 15-20 minutes until softened.
4. In a blender or food processor, combine the soaked chipotle peppers, chopped onion, garlic, tomato sauce, adobo sauce, ground cumin, dried oregano, and a pinch of salt and pepper.
5. Blend the mixture until smooth, gradually adding some of the soaking liquid to achieve the desired consistency.
6. In a saucepan, heat the vegetable oil over medium heat. Pour the blended sauce into the pan and simmer for about 10-15 minutes, stirring occasionally, to develop the flavors.
7. Taste and adjust the seasoning with more salt and pepper if needed. Your smoky chipotle pepper sauce is now ready to add a fiery twist to your enchiladas.

Fiery Chicken Filling Options

When it comes to the filling for your spicy chipotle chicken enchiladas, you have the opportunity to infuse your dish with even more heat and flavor. Here are two fiery chicken filling variations to consider:

Option 1: Spicy Chipotle Shredded Chicken

- 2 cups cooked and shredded chicken (poached or rotisserie)
- 2-3 tablespoons smoky chipotle pepper sauce (from the previous recipe)
- 1/4 cup chopped fresh cilantro
- Salt and pepper to taste

Option 2: Salsa Verde Chipotle Chicken

- 2 cups cooked and shredded chicken (poached or rotisserie)
- 1/2 cup salsa verde (store-bought or homemade)
- 1-2 tablespoons smoky chipotle pepper sauce (adjust to your desired spice level)
- 1/4 cup chopped green onions
- Salt and pepper to taste

Assembly:

1. Preheat your oven to 350°F (175°C).
2. Warm the smoky chipotle pepper sauce over low heat while you prepare the tortillas.
3. Soften corn or flour tortillas by wrapping them in a damp paper towel and microwaving for 20-30 seconds.
4. In the center of each tortilla, place a portion of your chosen fiery chicken filling and roll it up tightly. Place the rolled enchiladas seam-side down in a baking dish.
5. Pour the warmed chipotle pepper sauce over the enchiladas, ensuring they are evenly coated.
6. Bake the enchiladas in the preheated oven for about 20-25 minutes, or until the sauce is bubbly and the flavors meld together.
7. Garnish with chopped cilantro or green onions before serving.

With the irresistible smokiness of the chipotle pepper sauce and the fiery kick of the chicken filling, these enchiladas are perfect for those who crave bold and exciting flavors.

Chapter 7: Healthy and Light Chicken Enchiladas

Whole Wheat Tortillas

For those seeking a healthier twist on traditional enchiladas, whole wheat tortillas provide a nutritious and hearty alternative. These tortillas offer a nutty flavor and a boost of fiber, making your enchiladas not only delicious but also wholesome:

Ingredients:

- 2 cups whole wheat flour
- 1/2 teaspoon salt
- 3/4 cup warm water
- 2 tablespoons olive oil

Instructions:

1. In a mixing bowl, combine the whole wheat flour and salt.
2. Gradually add the warm water and olive oil, mixing with a spoon until a dough forms.
3. Transfer the dough to a floured surface and knead it for a few minutes until smooth and elastic.
4. Divide the dough into equal-sized balls (usually about golf ball-sized).
5. Roll out each ball into a thin, round tortilla using a rolling pin.
6. Heat a non-stick skillet over medium heat. Cook each

tortilla for about 1-2 minutes on each side until lightly browned and cooked through.

7. Stack the cooked tortillas on a plate and cover them with a clean kitchen towel to keep them warm and soft.

Lean Chicken and Veggie Fillings

The lean chicken and veggie filling for your healthy and light chicken enchiladas brings together the goodness of lean protein and a rainbow of vegetables, making for a satisfying and nutritious meal:

Ingredients:

- 2 cups cooked and shredded lean chicken (grilled or poached)
- 1 cup diced bell peppers (assorted colors)
- 1 cup diced zucchini or yellow squash
- 1 cup diced tomatoes
- 1 cup chopped spinach or kale
- 1 teaspoon olive oil
- 1 teaspoon ground cumin
- Salt and pepper to taste

Assembly:

1. Preheat your oven to 350°F (175°C).
2. Warm the desired enchilada sauce (from previous chapters) over low heat while you prepare the tortillas.
3. Soften whole wheat tortillas by wrapping them in a damp paper towel and microwaving for 20-30 seconds.
4. In a skillet, heat olive oil over medium heat. Add diced bell peppers, zucchini or yellow squash, and a pinch of salt. Sauté for about 3-4 minutes until slightly softened.
5. Stir in diced tomatoes and chopped spinach or kale. Cook for an additional 2-3 minutes until the vegetables are

tender.

6. Add the cooked and shredded lean chicken to the skillet. Season with ground cumin, salt, and pepper. Toss the mixture to combine.
7. In the center of each tortilla, place a portion of the chicken and veggie filling and roll it up tightly. Place the rolled enchiladas seam-side down in a baking dish.
8. Pour the warmed enchilada sauce over the enchiladas, ensuring they are evenly coated.
9. Bake the enchiladas in the preheated oven for about 20-25 minutes, allowing the flavors to meld together.
10. Serve with a side of fresh salsa or a dollop of Greek yogurt for added freshness.

With whole wheat tortillas and a vibrant chicken and veggie filling, these enchiladas strike a perfect balance between wholesome ingredients and delightful flavors.

Chapter 8: Fusion Flavors: Asian-Inspired Chicken Enchiladas

Teriyaki Glaze

Infuse the delectable flavors of Asia into your enchiladas with a tantalizing teriyaki glaze. This sweet and savory glaze adds a unique twist to the traditional dish, creating a fusion of culinary worlds that is sure to delight your taste buds:

Ingredients:

- 1/2 cup soy sauce
- 1/4 cup water
- 3 tablespoons brown sugar
- 2 tablespoons honey
- 1 tablespoon rice vinegar
- 1 teaspoon grated fresh ginger
- 2 cloves garlic, minced
- 1 teaspoon cornstarch (optional, for thickening)

Instructions:

1. In a saucepan, combine soy sauce, water, brown sugar, honey, rice vinegar, grated ginger, and minced garlic.
2. Bring the mixture to a simmer over medium heat, stirring to dissolve the sugar.
3. If desired, mix the cornstarch with a small amount of water to create a slurry. Gradually add the slurry to the sauce, stirring constantly, until the sauce thickens.
4. Simmer the sauce for an additional 2-3 minutes to ensure

the flavors meld together.

5. Remove the sauce from heat and let it cool before using.

Asian Vegetable and Chicken Fillings

Combine the delightful textures and vibrant colors of Asian vegetables with succulent chicken to create a fusion of flavors that captivates your senses:

Ingredients:

- 2 cups cooked and shredded chicken (grilled or poached)
- 1 cup julienned carrots
- 1 cup thinly sliced bell peppers (assorted colors)
- 1 cup sliced snow peas or snap peas
- 1 cup chopped bok choy or baby spinach
- 2 tablespoons sesame oil
- 2 tablespoons soy sauce
- 1 teaspoon grated fresh ginger
- Salt and pepper to taste

Assembly:

1. Preheat your oven to 350°F (175°C).
2. Warm the teriyaki glaze over low heat while you prepare the tortillas.
3. Soften corn or flour tortillas by wrapping them in a damp paper towel and microwaving for 20-30 seconds.
4. In a skillet, heat sesame oil over medium heat. Add julienned carrots and thinly sliced bell peppers. Sauté for about 2-3 minutes until slightly softened.
5. Stir in sliced snow peas or snap peas and chopped Bok choy or baby spinach. Cook for an additional 1-2 minutes until the vegetables are vibrant and tender.
6. Add the cooked and shredded chicken to the skillet. Season

with soy sauce, grated ginger, salt, and pepper. Toss the mixture to combine.

7. In the center of each tortilla, place a portion of the chicken and Asian vegetable filling and roll it up tightly. Place the rolled enchiladas seam-side down in a baking dish.

8. Pour the teriyaki glaze over the enchiladas, ensuring they are evenly coated.

9. Bake the enchiladas in the preheated oven for about 20-25 minutes, allowing the flavors to meld together.

10. Garnish with chopped green onions and toasted sesame seeds before serving.

With the allure of teriyaki glaze and the enticing combination of Asian-inspired vegetables and chicken, these fusion enchiladas are a testament to the magic of culinary creativity.

Chapter 9: Mediterranean Twist: Greek Chicken Enchiladas

Tzatziki Sauce

Infuse the enchanting flavors of the Mediterranean into your enchiladas with the creamy and refreshing taste of tzatziki sauce. This Greek-inspired sauce adds a cool and tangy dimension to your dish, creating a fusion that transports your taste buds to the shores of the Aegean:

Ingredients:

- 1 cup Greek yogurt
- 1/2 cucumber, grated and drained
- 2 cloves garlic, minced
- 1 tablespoon extra-virgin olive oil
- 1 tablespoon freshly squeezed lemon juice
- 1 tablespoon chopped fresh dill
- Salt and pepper to taste

Instructions:

1. In a bowl, combine Greek yogurt, grated and drained cucumber, minced garlic, extra-virgin olive oil, lemon juice, and chopped fresh dill.
2. Stir the mixture until well combined.
3. Season with salt and pepper to taste.
4. Cover the tzatziki sauce and refrigerate it for at least 30 minutes before using.

Mediterranean-Inspired Chicken Filling

Take your taste buds on a journey to the Mediterranean coast with a filling that marries the vibrant flavors of Greece with succulent chicken:

Ingredients:

- 2 cups cooked and shredded chicken (grilled or poached)
- 1/2 cup crumbled feta cheese
- 1/4 cup chopped Kalamata olives
- 1/4 cup diced tomatoes
- 1/4 cup chopped fresh parsley
- 1 tablespoon extra-virgin olive oil
- 1 teaspoon dried oregano
- Salt and pepper to taste

Assembly:

1. Preheat your oven to 350°F (175°C).
2. Warm the tzatziki sauce over low heat while you prepare the tortillas.
3. Soften corn or flour tortillas by wrapping them in a damp paper towel and microwaving for 20-30 seconds.
4. In a bowl, combine the shredded chicken, crumbled feta cheese, chopped Kalamata olives, diced tomatoes, chopped fresh parsley, extra-virgin olive oil, dried oregano, salt, and pepper. Toss the mixture to combine.
5. In the center of each tortilla, place a portion of the Mediterranean-inspired chicken filling and roll it up tightly. Place the rolled enchiladas seam-side down in a baking dish.

6. Pour the warmed tzatziki sauce over the enchiladas, ensuring they are evenly coated.
7. Bake the enchiladas in the preheated oven for about 20-25 minutes, allowing the flavors to meld together.
8. Garnish with additional chopped fresh parsley and crumbled feta cheese before serving.

With the allure of tzatziki sauce and the harmonious blend of Mediterranean-inspired ingredients, these enchiladas offer a delightful fusion that celebrates the flavors of Greece.

Chapter 10: Sweet and Savory: Mango Salsa Chicken Enchiladas

Fresh Mango Salsa

Elevate your enchiladas with a burst of tropical sweetness and refreshing flavors from a delightful mango salsa. This fresh and vibrant salsa adds a touch of sunshine to your dish, creating a harmonious balance of sweet and savory:

Ingredients:

- 2 ripe mangoes, peeled, pitted, and diced
- 1/2 red onion, finely chopped
- 1 red bell pepper, finely chopped
- 1 jalapeño pepper, seeded and finely chopped
- 1/4 cup chopped fresh cilantro
- 2 tablespoons freshly squeezed lime juice
- Salt and pepper to taste

Instructions:

1. In a bowl, combine the diced mangoes, finely chopped red onion, finely chopped red bell pepper, finely chopped jalapeño pepper, chopped fresh cilantro, and freshly squeezed lime juice.
2. Stir the mixture until well combined.
3. Season with salt and pepper to taste.
4. Cover the mango salsa and refrigerate it for at least 30 minutes before using.

Sweet and Tangy Chicken Filling

Create a captivating contrast of flavors by combining succulent chicken with the tropical essence of mango salsa for a filling that's both sweet and tangy:

Ingredients:

- 2 cups cooked and shredded chicken (grilled or poached)
- 1 cup mango salsa (prepared from the previous recipe)
- 1/4 cup chopped fresh cilantro
- 1 tablespoon honey
- 1 teaspoon ground cumin
- Salt and pepper to taste

Assembly:

1. Preheat your oven to 350°F (175°C).
2. Soften corn or flour tortillas by wrapping them in a damp paper towel and microwaving for 20-30 seconds.
3. In a bowl, combine the shredded chicken, mango salsa, chopped fresh cilantro, honey, ground cumin, salt, and pepper. Toss the mixture to combine.
4. In the center of each tortilla, place a portion of the sweet and tangy chicken filling and roll it up tightly. Place the rolled enchiladas seam-side down in a baking dish.
5. Bake the enchiladas in the preheated oven for about 20-25 minutes, allowing the flavors to meld together.
6. Serve the enchiladas with a drizzle of additional mango salsa and a sprinkle of chopped fresh cilantro for an extra burst of freshness.

With the delectable sweetness of mango salsa and the harmonious blend of flavors in the chicken filling, these enchiladas offer a delightful juxtaposition that tantalizes your taste buds.

Chapter 11: Tex-Mex BBQ Chicken Enchiladas

Tangy BBQ Sauce

Infuse your enchiladas with the bold and smoky flavors of Tex-Mex barbecue sauce. This tangy and robust sauce adds a touch of Southern comfort to your dish, creating a fusion of culinary traditions that's sure to satisfy your cravings:

Ingredients:

- 1 cup ketchup
- 1/4 cup apple cider vinegar
- 1/4 cup brown sugar
- 2 tablespoons molasses
- 1 tablespoon Worcestershire sauce
- 1 teaspoon smoked paprika
- 1/2 teaspoon onion powder
- 1/2 teaspoon garlic powder
- 1/2 teaspoon ground cumin
- 1/4 teaspoon cayenne pepper (adjust to your desired spice level)
- Salt and pepper to taste

Instructions:

1. In a saucepan, combine ketchup, apple cider vinegar, brown sugar, molasses, Worcestershire sauce, smoked paprika, onion powder, garlic powder, ground cumin, cayenne

pepper, salt, and pepper.

2. Bring the mixture to a simmer over medium heat, stirring to dissolve the sugar.

3. Simmer the sauce for about 10-15 minutes, allowing the flavors to meld together and the sauce to thicken.

4. Taste and adjust the seasoning with additional salt, pepper, or cayenne pepper if needed.

5. Remove the sauce from heat and let it cool before using.

BBQ Chicken and Cheese Filling

Create a hearty and satisfying filling by combining the rich flavors of BBQ chicken and melted cheese, capturing the essence of Tex-Mex comfort food:

Ingredients:

- 2 cups cooked and shredded BBQ chicken (grilled or roasted)
- 1 cup shredded cheddar cheese or a blend of cheeses
- 1/4 cup diced red onion
- 1/4 cup chopped fresh cilantro
- Salt and pepper to taste

Assembly:

1. Preheat your oven to 350°F (175°C).
2. Warm the tangy BBQ sauce over low heat while you prepare the tortillas.
3. Soften corn or flour tortillas by wrapping them in a damp paper towel and microwaving for 20-30 seconds.
4. In a bowl, combine the shredded BBQ chicken, shredded cheddar cheese, diced red onion, chopped fresh cilantro, salt, and pepper. Toss the mixture to combine.
5. In the center of each tortilla, place a portion of the BBQ chicken and cheese filling and roll it up tightly. Place the rolled enchiladas seam-side down in a baking dish.
6. Pour the warmed BBQ sauce over the enchiladas, ensuring they are evenly coated.
7. Bake the enchiladas in the preheated oven for about 20-25 minutes, allowing the flavors to meld together.

8. Garnish with additional chopped fresh cilantro before serving.

With the savory tang of BBQ sauce and the comforting combination of BBQ chicken and melted cheese, these enchiladas offer a Tex-Mex twist that's perfect for indulging in rich and satisfying flavors.

Chapter 12: Breakfast Enchiladas: Cheesy Chicken and Egg

Scrambled Egg and Chicken Filling

Start your day with a delicious and hearty breakfast twist on enchiladas, combining the comforting flavors of scrambled eggs and chicken for a satisfying morning meal:

Ingredients:

- 6 large eggs
- 1 cup cooked and shredded chicken (rotisserie or leftover)
- 1/2 cup shredded cheddar cheese or Mexican blend cheese
- 1/4 cup diced green bell pepper
- 1/4 cup diced red onion
- 2 tablespoons chopped fresh parsley or chives
- Salt and pepper to taste

Instructions:

1. In a bowl, whisk the eggs until well beaten. Season with salt and pepper.
2. In a non-stick skillet over medium heat, scramble the eggs until they are just cooked through. Remove from heat and set aside.
3. In a bowl, combine the scrambled eggs, shredded chicken, shredded cheddar cheese, diced green bell pepper, diced red onion, and chopped fresh parsley or chives. Toss the mixture to combine.
4. Taste and adjust the seasoning with additional salt and

pepper if needed.

Breakfast-Inspired Sauces

Elevate your breakfast enchiladas with flavorful sauces that capture the essence of a hearty morning meal:

Option 1: Creamy Sausage Gravy Sauce

- 1/2 pound breakfast sausage
- 2 tablespoons all-purpose flour
- 2 cups milk
- Salt and pepper to taste

Option 2: Roasted Tomato and Salsa Verde Sauce

- 1 cup roasted tomatoes (canned or homemade)
- 1/2 cup salsa verde (store-bought or homemade)
- 1 teaspoon ground cumin
- Salt and pepper to taste

Assembly:

1. Preheat your oven to 350°F (175°C).
2. Soften corn or flour tortillas by wrapping them in a damp paper towel and microwaving for 20-30 seconds.
3. In the center of each tortilla, place a portion of the scrambled egg and chicken filling and roll it up tightly. Place the rolled enchiladas seam-side down in a baking dish.
4. Choose your desired breakfast-inspired sauce and warm it over low heat.
5. Pour the warmed sauce over the enchiladas, ensuring they are evenly coated.

6. Bake the enchiladas in the preheated oven for about 15-20 minutes, allowing the flavors to meld together and the enchiladas to heat through.
7. Garnish with additional chopped fresh parsley or chives before serving.

With the comforting combination of scrambled eggs and chicken, paired with your choice of breakfast-inspired sauces, these breakfast enchiladas offer a delightful and hearty way to start your day.

Chapter 13: Seafood Lovers' Delight: Creamy Seafood Enchiladas

Creamy Seafood Sauce

Indulge in the pleasures of the sea with luscious creamy seafood sauce that brings the flavors of the ocean to your enchiladas. This rich and decadent sauce pairs perfectly with shrimp and crab meat, creating a luxurious seafood experience:

Ingredients:

- 2 tablespoons butter
- 2 tablespoons all-purpose flour
- 1 cup seafood or fish broth
- 1 cup heavy cream
- 1/2 cup grated Parmesan cheese
- 2 tablespoons freshly squeezed lemon juice
- 1 teaspoon Old Bay seasoning (or seafood seasoning blend)
- Salt and white pepper to taste

Instructions:

1. In a saucepan, melt the butter over medium heat.
2. Add the flour to the melted butter, stirring constantly to create a smooth roux. Cook the roux for 1-2 minutes until it slightly deepens in color.
3. Gradually whisk in the seafood or fish broth, ensuring no lumps form.
4. Reduce the heat to low and add the heavy cream, grated Parmesan cheese, freshly squeezed lemon juice, Old Bay

seasoning, salt, and white pepper. Continue to whisk until the mixture thickens and coats the back of a spoon.

5. Simmer the sauce for about 5-7 minutes, allowing the flavors to meld together.

6. Taste and adjust the seasoning with additional salt, pepper, or Old Bay seasoning if desired.

Shrimp and Crab Meat Fillings

Create an enchanting seafood medley by combining succulent shrimp and delicate crab meat for a filling that's brimming with oceanic goodness:

Ingredients:

- 1 cup cooked and peeled shrimp, chopped
- 1/2 cup cooked crab meat, flaked
- 1/4 cup diced red bell pepper
- 1/4 cup diced celery
- 1/4 cup chopped green onions
- 2 tablespoons chopped fresh parsley
- Salt and pepper to taste

Assembly:

1. Preheat your oven to 350°F (175°C).
2. Warm the creamy seafood sauce over low heat while you prepare the tortillas.
3. Soften corn or flour tortillas by wrapping them in a damp paper towel and microwaving for 20-30 seconds.
4. In a bowl, combine the chopped shrimp, flaked crab meat, diced red bell pepper, diced celery, chopped green onions, chopped fresh parsley, salt, and pepper. Toss the mixture to combine.
5. In the center of each tortilla, place a portion of the seafood filling and roll it up tightly. Place the rolled enchiladas seam-side down in a baking dish.
6. Pour the warmed creamy seafood sauce over the enchiladas, ensuring they are generously coated.

7. Bake the enchiladas in the preheated oven for about 20-25 minutes, allowing the flavors to meld together and the enchiladas to heat through.
8. Garnish with additional chopped fresh parsley before serving.

With the luxurious creaminess of the seafood sauce and the delectable combination of shrimp and crab meat, these enchiladas offer a seafood lover's dream come true.

Chapter 14: Vegan Variations: Plant-Based Chicken Enchiladas

Vegan Cheese and Sour Cream

Experience the joys of plant-based eating with vegan cheese and sour cream that bring a creamy and tangy twist to your enchiladas. These dairy-free alternatives offer a compassionate and delicious way to enjoy your favorite dish:

Ingredients:

- 1 cup cashews, soaked and drained
- 1/4 cup nutritional yeast
- 2 tablespoons freshly squeezed lemon juice
- 2 cloves garlic
- Salt and pepper to taste
- Water (for blending)

Instructions:

1. In a blender or food processor, combine soaked cashews, nutritional yeast, freshly squeezed lemon juice, garlic cloves, salt, and pepper.
2. Blend the mixture, gradually adding water until you achieve a smooth and creamy consistency similar to sour cream.
3. Taste and adjust the seasoning with additional salt, pepper, or lemon juice if desired.
4. Cover the vegan sour cream and refrigerate it until ready to use.

Plant-Based Chicken Alternatives

Create a satisfying and flavorful filling by using plant-based chicken alternatives, offering a cruelty-free and delicious option for your enchiladas:

Ingredients:

- 2 cups shredded plant-based chicken (e.g., soy-based, seitan, or jackfruit)
- 1/2 cup diced bell peppers (assorted colors)
- 1/4 cup diced red onion
- 1/4 cup corn kernels (fresh, frozen, or canned)
- 1/4 cup chopped fresh cilantro
- 1 tablespoon olive oil
- 1 teaspoon ground cumin
- Salt and pepper to taste

Assembly:

1. Preheat your oven to 350°F (175°C).
2. Soften corn or flour tortillas by wrapping them in a damp paper towel and microwaving for 20-30 seconds.
3. In a skillet, heat olive oil over medium heat. Add diced bell peppers and diced red onion. Sauté for about 2-3 minutes until slightly softened.
4. Stir in corn kernels and shredded plant-based chicken. Cook for an additional 2-3 minutes until the mixture is heated through.
5. Season the filling with ground cumin, salt, and pepper. Toss the mixture to combine.
6. In the center of each tortilla, place a portion of the plant-

based chicken filling and roll it up tightly. Place the rolled enchiladas seam-side down in a baking dish.

7. Pour your choice of enchilada sauce (from previous chapters) over the enchiladas, ensuring they are evenly coated.
8. Bake the enchiladas in the preheated oven for about 20-25 minutes, allowing the flavors to meld together and the enchiladas to heat through.
9. Serve with a dollop of vegan sour cream and a sprinkle of chopped fresh cilantro for a delightful finishing touch.

With the luscious creaminess of vegan cheese and sour cream and the savory goodness of plant-based chicken alternatives, these enchiladas offer a compassionate and flavorful option for those following a vegan lifestyle.

Chapter 15: Comfort Food: Mac and Cheese Chicken Enchiladas

Creamy Mac and Cheese Filling

Indulge in the ultimate comfort food fusion by combining the beloved flavors of mac and cheese with the satisfying goodness of chicken enchiladas. This creamy and cheesy filling will warm your heart and delight your taste buds:

Ingredients:

- 2 cups cooked macaroni pasta
- 1 cup shredded cheddar cheese or a blend of cheeses
- 1/2 cup grated Parmesan cheese
- 1 cup cooked and shredded chicken (rotisserie or leftover)
- 1/2 cup diced green bell pepper
- 1/4 cup diced red onion
- 1/4 cup chopped fresh parsley
- Salt and pepper to taste

Instructions:

1. In a large bowl, combine the cooked macaroni pasta, shredded cheddar cheese, grated Parmesan cheese, shredded chicken, diced green bell pepper, diced red onion, chopped fresh parsley, salt, and pepper. Toss the mixture to combine.
2. Taste and adjust the seasoning with additional salt and pepper if needed.

Cheesy Chicken Enchilada Bake

Transform your mac and cheese dreams into a comforting reality with this baked masterpiece that marries the flavors of mac and cheese with classic chicken enchiladas:

Ingredients:

- Prepared creamy mac and cheese filling (from previous recipe)
- Prepared enchilada sauce (from previous chapters)
- 8-10 corn or flour tortillas
- 1 cup shredded cheddar cheese or a blend of cheeses
- Additional chopped fresh parsley for garnish

Assembly:

1. Preheat your oven to 350°F (175°C).
2. Warm the desired enchilada sauce over low heat.
3. In a baking dish, spread a thin layer of enchilada sauce to coat the bottom.
4. Soften corn or flour tortillas by wrapping them in a damp paper towel and microwaving for 20-30 seconds.
5. Place a portion of the creamy mac and cheese filling in the center of each tortilla and roll it up tightly. Place the rolled enchiladas seam-side down in the baking dish.
6. Pour the warmed enchilada sauce over the enchiladas, ensuring they are generously coated.
7. Sprinkle the shredded cheddar cheese or blend of cheeses over the top.
8. Bake the enchiladas in the preheated oven for about 20-25 minutes, allowing the cheeses to melt and the flavors to

meld together.

9. Garnish with additional chopped fresh parsley before serving.

With the comforting embrace of creamy mac and cheese and the classic appeal of chicken enchiladas, these baked delights offer the perfect union of two beloved comfort foods.

Chapter 16: One-Pan Wonders: Skillet Chicken Enchiladas

Enchiladas in a Skillet

Simplify your cooking process without compromising on flavor by preparing your chicken enchiladas in a single skillet. This one-pan wonder offers a convenient and efficient way to enjoy your favorite dish with minimal fuss:

Ingredients:

- Prepared chicken filling of your choice (from previous chapters)
- Prepared enchilada sauce (from previous chapters)
- 8-10 corn or flour tortillas
- 1 cup shredded cheese (cheddar, Mexican blend, or vegan cheese)
- Optional toppings: diced tomatoes, chopped green onions, chopped fresh cilantro

Instructions:

1. In a large skillet, spread a thin layer of enchilada sauce to coat the bottom.
2. Soften corn or flour tortillas by wrapping them in a damp paper towel and microwaving for 20-30 seconds.
3. Place a portion of your preferred chicken filling in the center of each tortilla and roll it up tightly. Place the rolled enchiladas seam-side down in the skillet.
4. Pour the remaining enchilada sauce over the enchiladas,

ensuring they are evenly coated.

5. Sprinkle the shredded cheese over the top.

6. Cover the skillet with a lid or aluminum foil and cook over medium-low heat for about 15-20 minutes, allowing the cheeses to melt and the flavors to meld together.

7. Check periodically to ensure the enchiladas are heated through and the cheese is melted.

Quick and Easy Cleanup

Minimize cleanup time by using parchment paper or non-stick spray to line your skillet before assembling the enchiladas. This simple trick makes cleanup a breeze and allows you to focus on enjoying your delicious meal:

Instructions:

1. Before you start assembling the enchiladas in the skillet, line the skillet with parchment paper or generously coat it with non-stick cooking spray.
2. Follow the instructions for assembling the enchiladas as outlined above.
3. Once the enchiladas are cooked and ready to serve, simply lift the parchment paper or use a spatula to remove the enchiladas from the skillet. The parchment paper can be discarded, or the skillet can be easily cleaned with minimal effort.

With the convenience of skillet cooking and the option for quick and easy cleanup, these one-pan wonders offer a practical and enjoyable way to savor your favorite chicken enchiladas.

Chapter 17: Gluten-Free Options: Corn Tortilla Chicken Enchiladas

Corn Tortilla Wraps

Embrace a gluten-free lifestyle without compromising on flavor by using corn tortilla wraps for your chicken enchiladas. These naturally gluten-free tortillas offer a delicious and authentic base for your favorite dish:

Ingredients:

- 8-10 gluten-free corn tortillas (store-bought or homemade)
- Olive oil or cooking spray

Instructions:

1. Preheat a non-stick skillet over medium heat.
2. Lightly brush each side of a corn tortilla with olive oil or spray with cooking spray.
3. Place the oiled tortilla in the skillet and cook for about 20-30 seconds on each side, until it becomes pliable.
4. Repeat the process with the remaining tortillas, stacking them on a plate as you cook.

Gluten-Free Chicken Fillings

Create a scrumptious and gluten-free chicken filling that caters to your dietary needs, offering a satisfying and flavorful experience:

Ingredients:

- 2 cups cooked and shredded chicken (grilled or poached)
- 1/2 cup cooked quinoa or rice
- 1/4 cup diced green chilies
- 1/4 cup chopped fresh cilantro
- 1/4 cup diced red onion
- 1 tablespoon olive oil
- 1 teaspoon ground cumin
- Salt and pepper to taste

Assembly:

1. Preheat your oven to 350°F (175°C).
2. Warm your preferred enchilada sauce (from previous chapters) over low heat.
3. Soften the gluten-free corn tortillas by wrapping them in a damp paper towel and microwaving for 20-30 seconds.
4. In a bowl, combine the shredded chicken, cooked quinoa or rice, diced green chilies, chopped fresh cilantro, diced red onion, olive oil, ground cumin, salt, and pepper. Toss the mixture to combine.
5. In the center of each tortilla, place a portion of the gluten-free chicken filling and roll it up tightly. Place the rolled enchiladas seam-side down in a baking dish.
6. Pour the warmed enchilada sauce over the enchiladas, ensuring they are evenly coated.
7. Bake the enchiladas in the preheated oven for about 20-25 minutes, allowing the flavors to meld together and the enchiladas to heat through.
8. Garnish with additional chopped fresh cilantro before serving.

With the appeal of corn tortilla wraps and the satisfying blend of gluten-free chicken fillings, these enchiladas offer a delicious option for those following a gluten-free lifestyle.

Chapter 18: Leftover Magic: Rotisserie Chicken Enchiladas

Utilizing Rotisserie Chicken

Transform leftover rotisserie chicken into a delectable feast by incorporating it into your enchiladas. This clever use of pre-cooked chicken adds convenience and incredible flavor to your dish:

Ingredients:

- Leftover rotisserie chicken, shredded (about 2 cups)
- Prepared enchilada sauce (from previous chapters)
- 8-10 corn or flour tortillas
- Shredded cheese for topping (cheddar, Mexican blend, or vegan cheese)

Instructions:

1. Preheat your oven to 350°F (175°C).
2. Warm your preferred enchilada sauce over low heat.
3. Soften corn or flour tortillas by wrapping them in a damp paper towel and microwaving for 20-30 seconds.
4. In a bowl, combine the shredded rotisserie chicken with a portion of enchilada sauce, tossing to coat the chicken in the flavorful sauce.
5. In the center of each tortilla, place a portion of the sauced rotisserie chicken and roll it up tightly. Place the rolled enchiladas seam-side down in a baking dish.
6. Pour the remaining warmed enchilada sauce over the

enchiladas, ensuring they are evenly coated.

7. Sprinkle shredded cheese over the top.
8. Bake the enchiladas in the preheated oven for about 20-25 minutes, allowing the cheese to melt and the flavors to meld together.
9. Customize the dish by garnishing with leftover toppings or creating a new sauce (from previous chapters).

Flavorful Leftover Creations

Elevate your enchiladas with creative leftover creations, whether it's repurposing roasted vegetables or adding a unique twist with additional sauces:

Roasted Vegetable Variation:

Incorporate leftover roasted vegetables such as bell peppers, zucchini, or butternut squash into the enchilada filling for added flavor and texture.

Avocado Cream Sauce:

Blend ripe avocados with lime juice, garlic, cilantro, and a touch of dairy-free milk to create a creamy and refreshing sauce that complements the rich flavors of rotisserie chicken.

Pineapple Salsa:

Dice fresh pineapple and mix it with diced red onion, chopped cilantro, lime juice, and a pinch of chili flakes to create a vibrant and tangy salsa that pairs perfectly with the savory chicken.

With the magic of repurposing rotisserie chicken and creating flavorful leftover variations, these enchiladas offer a delightful way to enjoy a satisfying and inventive meal.

Chapter 19: Fresh and Homemade Tortillas

Step-by-Step Tortilla Making

Embark on a culinary adventure by crafting your own fresh and homemade tortillas, adding an authentic touch to your enchilada creation. Follow these simple steps to master the art of tortilla making:

Ingredients:

- 2 cups masa harina (corn flour)
- 1 1/2 cups warm water
- 1/2 teaspoon salt

Instructions:

1. In a mixing bowl, combine masa harina and salt.
2. Gradually add warm water while kneading the mixture with your hands until a soft dough forms.
3. Divide the dough into small golf ball-sized portions.
4. Preheat a griddle or non-stick skillet over medium heat.
5. Place a dough ball between two sheets of parchment paper or plastic wrap.
6. Use a tortilla press or a flat-bottomed heavy pan to flatten the dough ball into a thin, round tortilla.
7. Gently peel off the top layer of parchment paper and transfer the tortilla to the preheated griddle.
8. Cook the tortilla for about 1-2 minutes on each side, until it puffs up slightly and develops light brown spots.

9. Repeat the process with the remaining dough balls.

Elevating Your Enchiladas with Homemade Tortillas

Enhance your enchilada experience by using your freshly made homemade tortillas as the base for your dish. The delicate and authentic flavors of homemade tortillas will elevate your enchiladas to a new level of culinary excellence:

Instructions:

1. As you assemble your enchiladas (following any of the previous chapters' filling and sauce recipes), substitute the store-bought tortillas with your homemade tortillas.
2. Soften your homemade tortillas slightly by wrapping them in a damp paper towel and microwaving for 10-15 seconds to ensure they are pliable for rolling.
3. Fill each homemade tortilla with your chosen filling and roll it up tightly, then place it seam-side down in the baking dish.
4. Continue to follow the assembly and baking instructions from previous chapters, adjusting the cooking time if needed based on the thickness of your homemade tortillas.

By creating your own fresh and homemade tortillas, you're infusing your enchiladas with an authentic and artisanal touch.

Chapter 20: Dessert Enchiladas: Sweet Chicken and Chocolate

Decadent Dessert Fillings

Explore the realm of dessert enchiladas and indulge your sweet tooth with heavenly flavors. These decadent dessert fillings will take your taste buds on a delightful journey:

Sweet Chicken and Fruit Filling:

- 2 cups cooked and shredded chicken
- 1 cup diced fresh strawberries
- 1/2 cup diced mango
- 1/4 cup honey
- 1 teaspoon ground cinnamon
- Pinch of nutmeg

Indulgent Chocolate Sauces

Elevate your dessert enchiladas with rich and indulgent chocolate sauces that add an irresistible touch of sweetness:

Creamy Chocolate Sauce:

- 1 cup heavy cream
- 1 cup semisweet chocolate chips
- 2 tablespoons unsalted butter
- 1 teaspoon vanilla extract
- Pinch of salt

Spicy Chocolate Drizzle:

- 1/2 cup semisweet chocolate chips
- 1 tablespoon coconut oil
- 1/4 teaspoon ground cayenne pepper (adjust to your desired spice level)

Assembly:

1. Preheat your oven to 350°F (175°C).
2. In a bowl, combine the cooked and shredded chicken with diced fresh strawberries, diced mango, honey, ground cinnamon, and a pinch of nutmeg. Toss the mixture to combine.
3. Soften corn or flour tortillas by wrapping them in a damp paper towel and microwaving for 20-30 seconds.
4. In the center of each tortilla, place a portion of the sweet chicken and fruit filling and roll it up tightly. Place the

rolled enchiladas seam-side down in a baking dish.

5. Choose your preferred chocolate sauce (creamy or spicy) and warm it over low heat.

6. Pour the warmed chocolate sauce over the enchiladas, ensuring they are generously coated.

7. Bake the dessert enchiladas in the preheated oven for about 15-20 minutes, allowing the flavors to meld together and the enchiladas to heat through.

Creamy Chocolate Sauce:

1. In a saucepan, heat the heavy cream over medium heat until it begins to simmer.

2. Remove from heat and add the semisweet chocolate chips, unsalted butter, vanilla extract, and a pinch of salt.

3. Stir until the chocolate chips are fully melted and the sauce is smooth and creamy.

Spicy Chocolate Drizzle:

1. In a microwave-safe bowl, combine the semisweet chocolate chips and coconut oil.

2. Microwave in 15-second intervals, stirring in between, until the chocolate is fully melted and smooth.

3. Stir in the ground cayenne pepper to add a hint of spicy warmth.

With the tantalizing combination of sweet chicken and fruit filling and indulgent chocolate sauces, these dessert enchiladas offer a remarkable conclusion to your culinary journey.

In this culinary journey, we've embarked on a flavorful exploration of enchiladas, uncovering a wide array of variations that cater to different tastes, dietary preferences, and occasions. From classic chicken enchiladas to inventive twists and even dessert delights, we've ventured into the world of enchiladas and celebrated their versatility as a beloved and customizable dish.

Throughout this cookbook, we've dived into chapters dedicated to traditional flavors, innovative fusions, dietary adaptations, and even sweet indulgences. Each chapter offered a glimpse into the art of enchilada-making, guiding you through step-by-step instructions, ingredient lists, and assembly tips to create sensational dishes that bring joy to your table.

Whether you're a fan of rich and hearty sauces, a lover of spice and smokiness, or someone who enjoys the comfort of creamy textures, there's an enchilada variation tailored just for you. These recipes have encouraged you to experiment, get creative, and embrace the joy of cooking as you craft delicious meals that satisfy your cravings and impress your loved ones.

As you close the pages of this cookbook, remember that the world of enchiladas is a canvas for your culinary imagination. Feel free to mix and match fillings, sauces, and toppings, and don't be afraid to add your own personal flair to each dish. With enchiladas, the possibilities are endless, and your kitchen becomes a realm of flavor exploration.

Thank you for joining us on this journey through the tantalizing world of enchiladas. May your cooking endeavors continue to bring you delight, satisfaction, and the joy of sharing wonderful meals with those you hold dear. Happy cooking!